ARBOR DAY

Fulton Books, Inc.
Meadville, PA

Published by Fulton Books 2021

ISBN 978-1-64952-094-4 (paperback)
ISBN 978-1-63860-445-7 (hardcover)
ISBN 978-1-64952-095-1 (digital)

Printed in the United States of America

ARBOR DAY

MARTIN J. SMOUSE

Here is some history
That not many may know.
It's a story that happened
Many years ago.

1

It happened way back
In 1854
When a man and his wife
Went west to explore.

ARBOR
DAY

2

They packed up their belongings
And tied them real tight,

Said goodbye to their friends,
And drove out of sight.

On your way out west,
To stake out a claim,
You took note
That the scenery
Wasn't looking the same.

J. Sterling Morton,
Would you have ever guessed
The things that you'd start
By moving out west?

When arriving in Nebraska,
You found it quite odd
To find the tallest thing growing
Was flat grassy sod.

WELCOME TO NEBRASKA

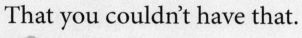

Yes, the land that you found
Was barren and flat.
And, Caroline, and you knew
That you couldn't have that.

Besides the lack
Of the beauty of trees,
There was a need
That was greater.
Yes, stronger indeed!

The soil was shifting,
Being blown all around.
They had to find something
To hold it down.

The answer was as plain
As the nose on your face.
They'd plant trees
To block the wind
To keep the soil in place.

13

The both of you knew
With the right kind of power
That you could change that
By planting trees, shrubs, and flowers.

So as the editor of Nebraska's
First newspaper post,
You were driven and determined
To give it your most.

The forum—your press,
You typed out a plea.
Everyone in town
Must plant a new tree!

The cry went out
For miles around,
And soon there were trees
Planted all over town.

With the problems all solved
And trees on the rise,
A holiday was in order,
A celebration,
And a prize.

So on January 4, 1872,
A holiday was proposed,
For both me and you.

Governor Robert W. Furnas
Took his pen from his vest,
And from that point on,
It is history at best.

"Arbor Day"
Was proclaimed,
The last Friday in April,
The day people plant
Oaks, pines, and maples.

So on this Arbor Day,
Won't you answer the plea?
With shovel in hand,
Let's go plant a tree.

About the Author

Martin Smouse, retired elementary school teacher, lives on the beautiful Space Coast in Rockledge, Florida, with his wife, Susan. In his spare time, he likes to spend time with his children, Hannah and Ben, Adam, Miranda, and friends doing different activities, such as bike riding, walking, camping, hiking, and especially attending church and fellowshipping with like-minded believers.

He thanks God for his many blessings, especially being able to communicate this story with people who share his beliefs that we need to do our part to protect our planet for our future generations.

Arbor Day is his first work that sat in a file of poems on his computer for fifteen years. He finally thought that instead of talking about having it published, he would take the next step and have it done. He hopes you enjoy the book and encourage your family and friends to dig up a copy and do their part to protect and beautify our environment.